Cambridge Primary
English
Second Edition
Workbook 5

Marie Lallaway

Series editors:
Christine Chen
Lindsay Pickton

Boost

HODDER EDUCATION
AN HACHETTE UK COMPANY

Registered Cambridge International Schools benefit from high-quality programmes, assessments and a wide range of support so that teachers can effectively deliver Cambridge Primary. Visit www.cambridgeinternational.org/primary to find out more.

Third-party websites, publications and resources referred to in this publication have not been endorsed by Cambridge Assessment International Education.

Acknowledgements
The Publishers would like to thank the following for permission to reproduce copyright material. Every effort has been made to trace or contact all copyright holders, but if any have been inadvertently overlooked, the Publishers will be pleased to make the necessary arrangements at the first opportunity.

Text acknowledgements
p. 22 © Edward Harrington; **p. 26** *The Wind* by James Reeves © James Reeves, 2009, published by Faber & Faber, reproduced by kind permission of David Higham Associates; **pp. 28, 31** Kingfisher *Young People's Book of Oceans*. First published by Kingfisher Publications Plc 1997, an imprint of Pan Macmillan. Reproduced by permission of Macmillan Publishers International Limited. Copyright © Macmillan Children's Books, 1997; **pp. 36, 38–39** From *The Invention of Hugo Cabret* by Brian Selznick. Copyright © 2007 by Brian Selznick. Reprinted by permission of Scholastic Inc. **pp. 44, 45, 46, 47** *The Seven Voyages of Sinbad the Sailor* by Kelley Townley, illustrated by Anja Gram. © Harpendore 2016. Reproduced with kind permission of Harpendore; **pp. 50–51** © The Roald Dahl Story Company Limited, adapted by Richard George; **pp. 53, 55–56, 59** © The Roald Dahl Story Company Limited; **p. 61** *Mother to Son* by Langston Hughes © Langston Hughes, 1994, published by Alfred A Knopf Inc, reproduced by kind permission of David Higham Associates; **pp. 63–64** © *The Lady of Shalott* (1832) by Alfred, Lord Tennyson.

Photo acknowledgements
p. 8 *bl* © Natalya Berezovskaya/Adobe Stock Photo; **p. 12** *cr* © CDK Productions/Adobe Stock Photo; **p. 13** *tl, cr,* **p. 19** *tl, cr* **p. 27** *tl, cr,* **p. 34** *tl, cr,* **p. 41** *tl, cr,* **p. 49** *tl, cr,* **p. 60** *tl, cr,* **p. 66** *tl, cr,* **p. 72** *tl, cr* © Stocker Team/Adobe Stock Photo; **p. 14** *tr* © NASA Photo/Alamy Stock Photo; **p. 17** *tr* © LMK Media/Alamy Stock Photo; **p. 21** *cr* © Andrey Popov/Adobe Stock Photo; **p. 29** © Save Jungle/Adobe Stock Photo; **p. 29** *br* © Neilras/Adobe Stock Photo; **p. 35** *cc,* **p.41** *tr* © Steshnikova/Adobe Stock Photo; **p. 62** *cr* © Stefa Notermanini/Adobe Stock Photo; **p. 67** *tr* © Kara/Adobe Stock Photo.

t = top, *b* = bottom, *l* = left, *r* = right, *c* = centre

Although every effort has been made to ensure that website addresses are correct at the time of going to press, Hodder Education cannot be held responsible for the content of any website mentioned in this book. It is sometimes possible to find a relocated web page by typing in the address of the home page for a website in the URL window of your browser.

Hachette UK's policy is to use papers that are natural, renewable and recyclable products and made from wood grown in well-managed forests and other controlled sources. The logging and manufacturing processes are expected to conform to the environmental regulations of the country of origin.

Orders: please contact Hachette UK Distribution, Hely Hutchinson Centre, Milton Road, Didcot, Oxfordshire, OX11 7HH. Telephone: +44 (0)1235 827827. Email education@hachette.co.uk. Lines are open from 9 a.m. to 5 p.m., Monday to Saturday, with a 24-hour message-answering service. You can also order through our website: www.hoddereducation.com

© Marie Lallaway 2021

First published in 2021 by
Hodder Education
An Hachette UK Company
Carmelite House
50 Victoria Embankment
London EC4Y 0DZ

www.hoddereducation.com

Impression number   10 9 8 7 6 5 4 3 2 1
Year   2025 2024 2023 2022 2021

Cover illustration by Lisa Hunt

Illustrations by James Hearne, Natalie Hinrichsen, Tamsin Hinrichsen and Vian Oelofsen

Typeset in FS Albert 17/19 by IO Publishing CC

Printed in the United Kingdom

A catalogue record for this title is available from the British Library.

ISBN 9781398300330

MIX
Paper from
responsible sources
FSC™ C104740

Contents

Note to teachers: This Workbook should be used alongside the *Cambridge Primary English Learner's Book 5*. Learners should complete the activities in the Learner's Book theme first. For complete coverage of the Cambridge Primary English Stage 5 curriculum framework, the Workbook cannot be used in isolation and must be used alongside the Learner's Book. The *Self-check* chart at the end of each unit in this Workbook refers to objectives covered in both the Learner's Book and Workbook units. Support for the Learner's Book and Workbook (including activity answers) can be found in the *Cambridge Primary English Teacher's Guide 5*.

Why Cockerels Crow (Part 1): A fable from Malawi

 1   Read this Malawian fable again.

Why Cockerels Crow

Everyone **admired** Cockerel because he had a bright red spiky **comb** on top of his head. You could see the red spikes from miles away. He told everyone that the red spikes were like flames that could set everything on fire with just one touch! Nobody wanted Cockerel to set things on fire, so they did everything they could to be friendly and **respectful** towards him. Cockerel loved everyone helping him, especially when they did his **chores** for him. The first time, Hyena ploughed his field for him for free! Cockerel sat in the shade and watched, without a care in the world. Cockerel was sitting with his feet up on an old table under the trees.

Glossary

admired: respected and approved of

comb: a soft, red growth on a chicken's head

respectful: showing admiration for someone or something

chores: jobs around the house that need doing regularly

2   Underline the sentences in the story extract that show you:
- Cockerel is lazy
- Hyena is a hard worker
- the other animals are scared of Cockerel.

3   On a separate sheet of paper, copy and complete the table to give your opinion about the characters in the story extract. Find and copy a quotation to show where you have found this implicit meaning. An example has been done for you.

Implicit information about a character	Which character behaves this way?	Quotation as evidence
lazy		
untruthful		
scared	Hyena	Nobody wanted Cockerel to set things on fire, so they did everything they could to be friendly and respectful.
hardworking		

4   Imagine that you are Cockerel. On a separate sheet of paper, write a paragraph about yourself, explaining why you think it's okay for others to do all of your chores.

Why Cockerels Crow (Part 2): A fable from Malawi

 Tick to show whether each sentence contains a fact or an opinion.

Sentence		Fact	Opinion
a	A male chicken is called a cockerel.		
b	The sky looks amazing this evening.		
c	It was the most exciting football match I'd ever played.		
d	After the concert, we walked home through the park.		
e	Tomorrow is Tuesday.		

 Which information in the passage below is fact and which is opinion? Underline the facts and circle the opinions.

> The fable is great. It's called *Why Cockerels Crow*. It's a fable from Malawi. The two main characters are Hyena and Cockerel. Cockerels crow because they like to wake people in the morning!

3 Write sentences about each picture. Each sentence must contain a fact and an opinion. Underline the opinions.

For example: *The moon is a <u>beautiful</u> crescent shape tonight.*

Why Monkeys live in Trees: A fable from South Africa

1 Proofread this extract from the fable *Why Monkeys live in Trees.* Find and correct seven mistakes. Rewrite the extract on a separate sheet of paper using the correct capital letters and punctuation.

many hours later Lioness woke up as she was trembling like a leaf. The son had gone down, the wind was blowing a harsh wind and Monkey was knowhere to be seen. lioness tried to stand up, but she couldn't? She looked at her tail and saw that it was tied around the tree in a big bow

2 Read this extract from the South African fable *Why Monkeys live in Trees,* and answer the questions.

Lioness was hunting all day, but luck was not on her side. For hours, she stalked prey and pounced and leapt, but caught nothing. She was so hungry and annoyed that she hadn't caught anything. It was a boiling hot day and the **fleas** in her fur were **working overtime**!

They wouldn't stop biting her and she could feel them running along her tail. She tried to flick her tail, but it wasn't any good! The fleas were making her beautiful coat and tail look patchy as her fur was falling out in **clumps**.

Retold by Marie Lallaway

Glossary

fleas: a small, jumping insect that feeds on other animals' blood

working overtime: doing something excessively

clumps: a group of things clustered together

a Which of the words below could be used to describe how Lioness is feeling in this part of the story? Colour the words.

(frustrated) (grumpy) (joyful) (famished) (patient) (gleeful) (desperate)

b Choose three of the feelings above and explain how you know that Lioness feels this way. For example: *Lioness feels _____ because she is _____.*

_____

_____

_____

_____

3 Imagine that you are a lion hunting prey. On a separate sheet of paper, write a paragraph to explain how you move and what you see, hear and feel.

Include interesting vocabulary such as verbs like *stalk* and *creep* or adjectives like *timid* and *silent*.

The First Sunrise: A fable from Australia

 Rewrite the complex (multi-clause) sentences below, adding commas correctly. An example has been done for you.

a *The explorers had been lost in the Australian desert for several days⊙ walking in circles⊙ not knowing where to go.*

b The kangaroos were so happy without hesitation they jumped straight into the lake.

_____

_____

_____

c Howling like a wolf tearing the leaves from branches the wind was growing stronger every moment.

_____

_____

 a Using your imagination, write a list of verbs that could be used to describe what might happen in the picture. For example: *paddle, row, tumble.*

_____

_____

_____

_____

b Use a thesaurus to find and write more words with similar meanings to the ones you have written above. For example: *tumble – drop, tilt, roll.*

_____

_____

 On a separate sheet of paper, write sentences to describe what might happen using complex (multi-clause) sentences to create a sense of danger.
For example: *The small boat was too close to the edge of the falls, pulled by the powerful current, teetering on the brink.*

The Elephant who lost his Patience: A fable from India

 1 Read this extract from the Indian fable *The Elephant who lost his Patience*. Notice how the writer carefully chooses words to show how Ant behaves.

> This insect didn't like anyone in the jungle. Ant was <u>tiny</u>, but he had small, <u>angry</u> eyes and would wave his pincers at anyone that went past. All day, every day, Ant would tease the monkeys about their ears, the oxpeckers about eating ticks and flies from other animals, the baboons for their brightly coloured faces, and the lions about their <u>frizzy</u> manes. All of them threatened him, and Ant ran away as he knew they would hurt him if they got too close. The one that Ant teased the most was King Elephant. It was such a piece of cake! King Elephant was so calm and quiet that Ant knew he wouldn't do or say anything. 'Look at those ridiculous ears! They are so big that when you flap them, a tornado starts,' taunted Ant as he sat on a rock watching King Elephant take his daily shower in the waterfall. King Elephant was hurt by the comments, but he pretended he hadn't heard.

a Which words tell you that Ant is unkind.

b Which words tell you that Ant is cowardly?

c Which adjectives have been used to describe the appearance of:

- the lions?
- the baboons?

d Find the three adjectives that have been underlined. Replace each one with a different adjective.

Use a separate sheet of paper to answer questions **a–d**.

2 Write three things that King Elephant might be thinking or feeling during the moments described in the fable extract.

3 Match these idiomatic phrases (underlined) with their meanings. An example has been done for you.

a | I learned how to use a computer <u>one step at a time</u>.

b | Can you <u>walk me through</u> that?

c | I'm finding your explanation <u>hard to</u> <u>swallow</u>.

d | He's a really <u>bright spark</u>.

e | <u>Break a leg</u>!

f | You'll need to take what she says <u>with</u> <u>a pinch of salt</u>.

g | They gave us quite <u>a frosty reception</u>.

h | The police will <u>get to the bottom of</u> this mystery.

i | She's still <u>sitting on the fence</u> about your idea.

He is very clever.

They greeted us coldly.

Can you show me how to do that?

I did it slowly and carefully.

She exaggerates a lot.

I don't really believe you.

Good luck!

She can't make up her mind.

They will find out what happened.

4 Choose three of your favourite idiomatic phrases from question 3 above and write your own sentences using them.

_____

_____

_____

5 Find five examples of idiomatic phrases from your own country. Write a conversation that includes these phrases.
For example: 'Let's see if we can mend this bicycle. It's not rocket science, you know!' said Lola.

_____

_____

_____

_____

_____

_____

The Lion with the Red Eyes: A fable from Somalia

1 Choose the correct comparative or superlative form of each adverb to complete the sentence.

The **comparative** form is where only two things are being compared. The **superlative** form compares more than two things of the same type.

   a   Cuka was the _____ of all the lions in the jungle. (**louder / loudest**)

   b   Lingo moves _____ than Cuka. (**more slowly / most slowly**)

   c   Dido ran fast, but Cuka ran _____ because he reached the dragon first. (**faster / fastest**)

   d   Cuka fought _____ than the dragon. (**better / best**)

2 a   Complete this table to show the comparative and superlative form of each adverb.

Positive	Comparative	Superlative
badly		
much		
little		
well		
joyfully		
fast		
far		

   b   On a separate sheet of paper, write sentences for each adverb using the comparative and superlative forms.

3 Read this extract from the Somalian fable, *The Lion with the Red Eyes*, and answer the questions on a separate sheet of paper.

By the light of the village fires, he saw the dragon's gold body of scales, the huge **talons** outstretched and the massive jagged yellow and green teeth sticking out of the fire-spreading mouth. Without a second thought, Cuka ran like the wind and charged down the mountain. His booming roar was so loud and **ferocious** that the dragon got a terrible fright and flew off into the night sky.

   a   Describe the mood that the writer has created. Use words from the text to support your opinion.

   b   Which words tell you that Cuka is fearless?

   c   Which words tell you how fast Cuka can run?

Glossary
talons: claws
ferocious: cruel and violent

4 Underline the adverbial phrases in the sentences below that tell you *where* something happened. The first one has been done for you.

   a Cuka stopped <u>at the edge of the steep cliff</u>.

   b The tiger moved between the tall trunks of the forest trees.

   c High above the forest floor, the orangutans fed and played and slept.

   d Small creatures were sleeping inside delicate nests.

5 Underline the adverbial phrases in the sentences below that tell you *how* something was done. The first one has been done for you.

   a The monkeys shrieked a warning, <u>piercing the night's silence</u>.

   b A bear patrolled the forest tracks, silently searching for prey.

   c Sliding silently and cautiously, a snake moved across the forest floor.

   d Men tramped along the trail, snapping sticks and chopping back bushes.

6 On a separate sheet of paper, write four sentences using adverbial phrases of place (where) and manner (how). Use the table below to help you. Some examples have been done for you.

> *Small children played beside the busy road, not thinking about the dangers.*

> *Not thinking about the dangers, small children played beside the busy road.*

Main clause	Adverbial phrase of place (where)	Adverbial phrase of manner (how)
small children played	from the waterhole	not thinking about the dangers
colourful parrots were perched	beside the busy road	hanging their heads and straining with the weight
elephants drank deeply	through the narrow streets of the town	enjoying the cool freshness
donkeys pulled carts	high in the canopy of the trees	gripping firmly and chattering loudly

The Broath with the Rocks: A fable from Scotland

 Proofread this extract from the Scottish fable *The Broath with the Rocks*.

a Check that full stops and commas have been used correctly. Cross out full stops and commas that are in the wrong place and add any that are missing.

b Check spellings and grammar. Cross out any errors and write the correct words above the error. Some examples have been done for you.

passed

Curiosity got the better of the old man and he past the salt and pepper mills out to the cook through the window. 'Do you know I once made the perfect rock broath with cabbage and karrots!'

'I have fresh cabbage and carrots?' cooled the old man. 'There … two your left.'

'… and i am sure that it had onions and **neeps** in as well, continued the traveller.

'Their on your right!' the old man pointed excitedly threw the window.

After adding lots of delicious ingredients, the old man could smell the **sumptuous** flavours floating through the open window?

Glossary
neeps: turnips (Scottish)
sumptuous: splendid and delicious

2 Do you remember the ending? Write the final paragraph of the fable in your own words.

_____

_____

_____

_____

_____

_____

_____

_____

_____

_____

_____

Self-check

 I can do this.

 I can do this, but I need to keep trying.

 I can't do this yet.

What can I do?			
1 I can find explicit information in a text.			
2 I can tell the difference between a fact and an opinion.			
3 I can use implicit information to form opinions about characters.			
4 I can identify the mood of a setting.			
5 I can create a setting to convey a particular mood.			
6 I can build complex (multi-clause) sentences to create pace and excitement.			
7 I can use adverbs and adverbial phrases to add precision to my ideas.			
8 I can recognise some idioms and explain their meanings.			
9 I can proofread my writing for accuracy of punctuation and spelling.			

What do you need more help with? Write the number or numbers.

I need more help with:

_____

_____

What is a biography?

1 Read this biography about Mae Jemison, who made history when she became the first African-American astronaut.

Mae Jemison: Reach for the stars

On 12 September 1992, Mae Jemison became the first African-American woman to blast into outer space.

Mae was born on 17 October 1956 in Decatur, Alabama – the youngest of three children in her family. Mae loved to dance and was a talented ballerina, but she also loved to watch *Star Trek*, a TV series that included an African-American woman as a key figure on the spaceship in the programme. Mae was a bright student and she finished high school at only 16, instead of 18. Afterwards, she went to a top university in the USA. Later on, she trained to be a doctor and became a 'Flying Doctor' in East Africa.

In 1987, Mae was eventually chosen from 2 000 applicants to join NASA's space programme in Houston, Texas. Jemison finally realised her biggest dream in 1992, when she became an astronaut. Neil Armstrong (the first man to walk on the moon) said, 'She well and truly deserves this magnificent achievement.'

2 On a separate sheet of paper, copy and complete this table with examples of these features of a biography from the text.

Feature	Example from the text
Written in the third person	
An opening statement about the person	
Dates of important events in her life	
Facts	
Direct speech	

3 The first paragraph tells you why Mae Jemison is important. Write a sentence to describe what the other paragraphs are about.

Paragraph 2: _____

Paragraph 3: _____

4 Answer these questions about the biography on a separate sheet of paper.

a Why has the writer included information about a TV programme?

b How do you know that Mae was extraordinary as a child?

c Why has Neil Armstrong's comment been included?

Chronological order

1 Look back at the biography of Mae Jennison on page 14. Scan read to find and copy the adverbs and adverbial phrases of time that are used to organise the chronology of her life. For example:

Look carefully. Most of the adverbial phrases of time are used to start sentences but some of them are inside the sentences.

Paragraph 2: _Afterwards,_ _____

Paragraph 3: _____

2 Put these dates into chronological order, using a timeline or a list.

(2012) (6 February 1952) (1977) (2 June 1953) (8 May 1945)

(21 April 1926) (20 November 1947) (2002)

3 Find these features of a biography in the word search.

(fact) (date) (opinion) (statement) (chronological) (adverbs) (speech)

c	s	p	e	e	c	h	s	b
h	w	r	f	t	p	f	t	k
r	d	g	h	s	w	e	a	o
o	p	i	n	i	o	n	t	c
n	y	n	s	n	g	y	e	s
o	j	z	a	f	d	d	m	l
l	b	d	j	d	a	s	e	x
o	c	t	g	l	b	c	n	y
g	s	p	b	u	d	a	t	e
i	q	k	n	r	v	l	a	h
c	u	b	c	b	k	k	e	g
a	r	v	n	r	h	d	f	l
l	g	a	d	v	e	r	b	s

Writing to engage a reader

1 Change the word **nice** in the examples below for a more interesting adjective. An example has been done for you.

a nice dress   <u>a pretty dress</u> _____

a nice smell   _____

a nice castle   _____

a nice person   _____

a nice armchair   _____

a nice song   _____

2 Check the meanings of the words below and add the synonyms to the correct spider diagram.

Remember to record new words in your *Spelling log.*

(carefully)   (swiftly)   (cruelly)

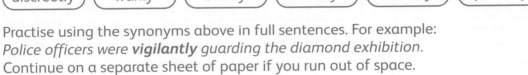

(callously) (vigilantly) (thoughtfully) (hurriedly) (hastily)

(discreetly) (warily) (briskly) (calmly) (brutally) (spitefully)

3 Practise using the synonyms above in full sentences. For example:
*Police officers were **vigilantly** guarding the diamond exhibition.*
Continue on a separate sheet of paper if you run out of space.

_____

_____

_____

_____

_____

_____

_____

_____

_____

_____

Using facts and opinions in biography texts

  Read this text about a famous British poet.

Perhaps one of the most famous British poets, playwrights and authors of current times is Dr Benjamin Zephaniah. Loved by the public and critics alike, Zephaniah's work crosses many class boundaries, and represents the modern face of urban Britain.

Born in Birmingham, which he refers to as the 'Jamaican capital of Europe', he left school at the age of 13, unable to read or write. He then went on to make music and write children's poetry books as well. His first children's book, *Talking Turkeys*, has been a huge inspiration for many young poets.

His poetry is a reflection of his surroundings and growing up with the music and poetry of Jamaica. He moved to London when he was 22 years old and had his first poetry book published in 1980. The book was so popular that there have been three editions so far. This book injected life into the British poetry scene. Suddenly, Benjamin was being chased by publishers that he had been turned down by 12 months earlier. They all wanted a piece of the pie.

The poet has often said that his mission in life is to fight the stereotypical image of poetry only being written for and by ancient professors in famous universities. For many, this image represents an alien and unfamiliar world, whereas the poet's own appeal, identity and persona are familiar, identifiable and based in reality for the majority of the population. He made poetry popular again and encouraged a whole new population of people who did not read books but who could see poetry live on stage or on TV. In 1991, over a period of 22 days, he performed on every continent.

Benjamin has won many awards and honorary degrees for his work. He is vegan and is known as a peace activist.

2 Answer these questions. Provide evidence from the text to support your answers.

   a How well did Dr Zephaniah do in school? _____

   b What talents has he developed since he left school? _____

   c Why were publishers suddenly interested in him? _____

   _____

   d Why does Dr Zephaniah fight the old-fashioned view of poetry?

   _____

3 Read the text again, and find quotes that mean:

   a everyone likes Dr Zephaniah's poetry: _____

   b is known or famous for: _____

4 Reread the first two paragraphs in the text. On a separate sheet of paper, find and write three facts and three opinions from these paragraphs.

Prefixes and suffixes

1 Sort the words below into three groups, according to their prefixes.

in	im	ir

visible   possible   expensive   responsible   secure

credible   mature   complete   mortal   active

patient   correct   regular   polite

2 Write the root words by removing the prefixes and/or suffixes from these words. An example has been done for you.

a   disagreeable   _agree_

b   dislike   _____

c   disgracefully   _____

d   illegally   _____

e   illogical   _____

f   beautiful   _____

g   unhappiness   _____

3 Practise doubling the consonant before adding the suffixes to these verbs by writing a sentence that includes each one. An example has been done for you.

a   travel   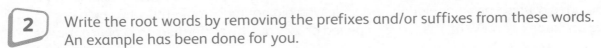 **travelling**: I will be **travelling** to my village with William.

b   plan   _____

c   flip   _____

d   swim   _____

e   begin   _____

f   prefer   _____

Unit 2 Non-fiction: Biography

Self-check

 I can do this.

 I can do this, but I need to keep trying.

 I can't do this yet.

What can I do?			
1 I can describe three features of a biography.			
2 I can explain the difference between facts and opinions.			
3 I can give an example of chronological order.			
4 I can use adverbs and adverbial phrases of time to show chronological order in my writing.			
5 I can describe two different ways of making a plan for writing.			
6 I can use a thesaurus to find synonyms for overused words.			
7 I can give examples of words with prefixes and words with suffixes.			
8 I can explain how the prefixes **im** and **il** change the meaning of words.			

 What do you need more help with? Write the number or numbers.

I need more help with:

_____

_____

Features of narrative poems

1   **a**   With your partner, read the poem aloud. Try to keep the rhythm of the poem as you read.

My Best Friend

I know my best friend in and out
She's always by my side
My parents sometimes holler and shout
When they see us playing inside

She helps me with my homework
And plays my favourite tunes
We always text and video chat
By then my bedtime looms

We watch movies under the covers
And can't stop giggling out loud
My parents take my best friend away
And tell me it's not allowed

Then one day, the dark clouds came
My best friend's battery died
I tried and tried to save her
But she just made a noise and sighed.

I am all alone now
My best friend is sadly no more
She was almost irreplaceable
But I can get another at the store

My mum says I need to play more
And spend time with real friends
But how do I play with people?
I need some time to mend

Next week, was sitting in my room
A knock upon the door
'Fancy a walk?' a small voice asked
'Yeah, sure,' I crossed the floor.

Now I have a real best friend
For walks, and talks and fun
We smile, we laugh and play outside
After all our homework's done.

By Rosemary Licciardi

b   In a narrative poem, there is a beginning, a middle and an end. Copy this table on a separate sheet of paper. Make notes about the progression of ideas in the poem above. Leave the third column blank for now.

	My Best Friend	The First Online Lesson
The beginning: Who are the main characters and where is the setting?		
The middle: What is the issue and how is it resolved?		
The end: What happens in the end of the poem?		
Can you retell what happens in the poem, in the correct order?		
How does the poet use personalisation and/or metaphors in this poem? Give examples.		

2 Read the poem, *The First Online Lesson*. Then, complete the table on page 20.

The First Online Lesson

I was wobbling like a jelly on a plate
I didn't know what to do
I sat with my earphones on
My hair combed flat as a pancake
Watching and waiting
Watching and waiting
Watching and waiting

Was I in the wrong place?
Was it the wrong time?
I checked my watch and the clock on the wall
Watching and waiting
Watching and waiting
Watching and waiting

Little beads of sweat trickling down my back
I saw my face red, like a tomato
A small box in front of me
Suddenly all my friends waving and smiling
Still watching and waiting
Watching and waiting
Watching and waiting

Their mouths opening and closing
Like baby birds about to be fed.
My tomato face looming
My teacher's eagle eyes staring at me
Watching and waiting
Watching and waiting
Watching and waiting

A small sign of hope
PUSH THE BUTTON it read in red
My teacher's talons pointing at something
Everyone still
Watching and waiting
Watching and waiting
Watching and waiting

The noise was like a crack of thunder in my ears
Why didn't you press the button?
My teacher demanded
But I was with my friends online and I didn't care
The lesson began and I was no longer
Watching and waiting
Watching and waiting
Watching and waiting

By Marie Lallaway

 3 Use this template to come up with ideas about a narrative poem. Remember that poems do not need to rhyme! In each box, think about what metaphors and figurative language you could use to make your poem more vivid, and make notes.

Beginning	Middle	End
Think about the setting and the characters.	Think about a problem and a resolution.	Think about how to bring the narrative to an end.

Finding out about characters

 1 Read these verses from the poem *The Bushrangers* aloud. This poem is about a famous Australian outlaw gang. The gang robbed banks and hid out in the countryside but, eventually, they were caught.

The Bushrangers

Four horseman rode out from the heart of the **range**,
Four horseman with **aspects** forbidding and strange.
They were booted and **spurred**, they were armed to the teeth,
And they frowned as they looked at the valley beneath,
As forward they rode through the rocks and the fern –
Ned Kelly, Dan Kelly, Steve Hart and Joe Byrne.

Through the **gullies and creeks** they rode silently down;
They stuck-up the station and raided the town;
They opened the safe and they looted the bank;
They laughed and were merry, they ate and they drank.
Then off to the ranges they went with their gold –
Oh! never were bandits more reckless and bold.

By Edward Harrington

Glossary
range: untamed open land
aspects: faces
spurred: spurs are sometimes worn by horse riders on their boots to direct the horse
gullies and creeks: rivers

2 Reread the poem *The Bushrangers*. Answer these questions.

a What do you learn about the characters in this narrative poem?

_____

b How do they look at the start of the poem? _____

c What are they wearing? _____

d How do they travel? _____

e How do they look after they rob the bank? _____

f Copy the words that are used to describe the setting of the poem.

_____

3 Does the writer of the poem approve or disapprove of the outlaws? Explain why you think this, using evidence from the poem.

_____

_____

Writing dialogue

 1 Which words in these sentences should not have apostrophes? Rewrite the incorrect words correctly.

a We have fish and chip's for this evening's supper.

_____

b Liam's book's were on the table where he'd left them.

_____

c I saw a chimpanzee and it's baby eating the zoo-keepers' lunches.

_____

2 Rewrite these sentences using as much contraction as possible. Draw arrows to show the contractions. For example:

*I **do** not know what **you have** done to these sandwiches.*

*I **don't** know what **you've** done to these sandwiches.*

a You should not talk with your mouth full or you will make a mess.

_____

b I shall bring my bike if you are able to bring yours too.

_____

c We had better not make too much noise or the neighbours will be annoyed.

_____

3 Find another contracted word to rhyme with each contraction below. For example: *can't* and *shan't*.

a won't _____   **b** couldn't _____   **c** would've _____

4 Use the contractions from question 3 on page 23 to write a simple poem using the names of people you know. For example:

> *I asked for help with my apostrophes*
> *and this is what people said to me:*
> *Mum said that she* **would've**
> *but she was doing yoga*
> *Dad said that he* **should've**
> *but he was …*
> *Brother said that …*

_____

_____

_____

_____

_____

_____

_____

5 Correctly add speech marks and a comma to each sentence below.

a I am going to ride my go-kart later said Pablo.

b Karla announced My pet hamster has just had four babies!

c I will take you swimming next week Ben Mum promised.

If the second part of the direct speech is a new sentence, it will start with a capital letter.

'Make sure you put on sunscreen,' said Dad. **'It's** *a very hot day.'*

But, if the second part of the direct speech is *not* a new sentence, it will start with a lower case letter.

'Mum,' asked Noor, **'what** *is that big box for?'*

6 Add the correct punctuation to the direct speech in each sentence below. Decide where you need to use speech marks, capital letters and commas.

a see this, aysha?' oliver called proudly it's the present my grandma gave me

b i think,' said ali i know of someone who may be able to help us

c you can trust me said Min. i'll be really careful.

What is a metaphor?

1 Add the name of a person you know to these sentences describing people.
For example:
Aroon is as calm as a waveless ocean.

_____ is a dazzling firework, full of surprises.

_____ works as hard as a busy honeybee.

_____ prowls the kitchen, a tiger searching for prey.

_____ has a voice like a whisper on a gentle breeze.

_____ sings as beautifully as a bird on a summer's eve.

_____ is a high voltage live-wire of electricity.

_____ is a fountain of knowledge.

_____ zooms around the playground like a high-speed racing car.

_____ is a bubbling ball of excitement.

2 Now decide which of the sentences above are similes and which are metaphors.
Write **S** for similes and **M** for metaphors next to the sentences.

3 Create your own metaphors to describe the objects in the picture below.

The mountains are _____

The lake's surface is _____

The trees are _____

The snow is _____

Personification

1 Read this poem and decide what the title should be.
Write the title on the line.

The _____

I can get through a doorway without any key,
And strip the leaves from the great oak tree.
I can drive storm-clouds and shake tall towers,
Or steal through a garden and not wake the flowers.
Seas I can move and ships I can sink;
I can carry a house-top or the scent of a **pink**.
When I am angry I can rave and riot;
And when I am **spent**, I lie quiet as quiet.

By James Reeves

Glossary
pink: a type of flower
spent: exhausted

2 Copy an example of personification in the poem above, which shows that the subject
of the poem can be:

a powerful: _____

_____

b gentle: _____

_____

c silent: _____

_____

d destructive: _____

_____

3 Create your own personification poem about the rain.

a First, write down all the things that the rain can do. For example: *soak, drop, drip, pour,
drench, wash, flood.*

_____

_____

b Then, think about how the rain would do these actions if it were a person.
For example:
*I **wash** the streets to make them clean and new.*
*When I am bored, I **drip and drizzle** all day long.*

Then write your poem on a separate sheet of paper.

Self-check

 I can do this.

 I can do this, but I need to keep trying.

 I can't do this yet.

What can I do?			
1 I can understand and explain the story of a narrative poem.			
2 I can comment on characters in narrative poems.			
3 I can identify rhythm and rhyme in lines of poetry.			
4 I can read poems aloud with accuracy and expression, including gestures and movement.			
5 I can identify and create metaphors and personification.			
6 I can plan and write poems that tell stories.			
7 I can choose verbs and adjectives to develop characters.			
8 I can accurately punctuate dialogue.			
9 I can accurately use apostrophes for contractions.			
10 I can listen to what others say and give my opinion in response.			

What do you need more help with? Write the number or numbers.

I need more help with:

_____

_____

What is an information text?

1 Skim read this information text to find out what it is about.

A glacier is a huge mass of ice that moves slowly over land. The term **glacier** comes from the French word *glace* (glah-say), which means **ice**. Glaciers are often called **rivers of ice**. During the Pleistocene Ice Age, nearly one-third of the Earth's land was covered by glaciers. Today, about one-tenth of the Earth's land is covered by glacial ice. Glaciers fall into two groups: alpine glaciers and ice sheets.

Alpine glaciers form on mountain sides and move downward through valleys. Sometimes, alpine glaciers create or deepen valleys by pushing dirt, soil, and other materials out of their way. Alpine glaciers are found in high mountains of almost every continent. The Gorner Glacier in Switzerland and the Furtwängler Glacier in Tanzania are both typical alpine glaciers. Alpine glaciers are also called valley glaciers or mountain glaciers.

Ice sheets, unlike alpine glaciers, are not limited to mountainous areas. They form broad domes and spread out from their centres in all directions. As ice sheets spread, they cover everything around them with a thick blanket of ice, including valleys, plains, and even entire mountains. The largest ice sheets, called continental glaciers, spread over vast areas. Today, continental glaciers cover most of Antarctica and the island of Greenland.

2 Tick three boxes to show what the extract is about.

- How glaciers are formed ◯
- Types of glaciers ◯
- Damage done by glaciers ◯
- Where to find glaciers ◯
- Why we need glaciers ◯

3 **a** Tick to show which features of an information text can be found in the extract above. Add a cross to show which features are missing.

a title	
an introduction	
sub-headings	
sections	
facts	
bullet points	

b Write your own suggestions for the features that are missing. Use a separate sheet of paper.

Differences between information and explanation texts

1 Add the correct words from the boxes below to complete the passage.

(combined) (non-chronological) (process) (information) (chronological)

Information texts can be ⬭⬭⬭⬭⬭ but explanation texts are usually

⬭⬭⬭⬭⬭ because they explain a ⬭⬭⬭⬭⬭ in the order that

it happens. Both types of texts can be ⬭⬭⬭⬭⬭ to give a wider range of

⬭⬭⬭⬭⬭ about a topic.

2 Explanation texts usually give information about five things. Complete these words to show these things. An example has been done for you.

a What

b Wh_____

c Wh_____

d H_____

e Wh_____

3 Improve the passage below by changing the underlined words for a more precise word from the boxes. An example has been done for you.

(created) (trapped) (contaminated) (resource) (source) (pollutants)

The most important <u>thing</u> (resource) provided by glaciers is freshwater. Many

rivers are fed by the melting ice of glaciers. The Gangotri Glacier, one of the largest

glaciers in the Himalayan Mountains, is the <u>start</u> ⬭⬭⬭⬭⬭ of the Ganges

River. The Ganges is the most important source of

freshwater and electricity in India and Bangladesh.

Electricity is <u>made</u> ⬭⬭⬭⬭⬭ by dams

and hydroelectric power plants along the Ganges.

Some companies link glacial water to a clean,

fresh taste. Because water has been <u>held</u>

⬭⬭⬭⬭⬭ in the glacier for so

long, many people believe it has not been

<u>spoiled</u> ⬭⬭⬭⬭⬭ by the <u>dirtiness</u>

⬭⬭⬭⬭⬭ that other water is exposed to.

Writing an information text

 You are going to write a short information text about one of the following topics:

a   Your town or city

b   Your region or country

c   A famous national park in your country

d   A famous day or date in your culture.

Remember these key features that you should include:

- The main title that sums up the topic
- Headings and sub-headings to introduce the ideas in the paragraphs
- Paragraphs that divide and organise the information
- Bullet points to tell the reader the key information they need to know
- Photos, drawings and diagrams help to make the text easier to understand
- Research on the topic from the internet and books, as well as from friends and family.

Use a mind map to plan your content ideas before you write your information text.

Sub-heading 1:

_____

Key words: _____

_____

_____

Sub-heading 2:

_____

Key words: _____

_____

_____

_____

_____

_____

_____

_____

Main title:

_____

_____

Sub-heading 3:

_____

Key words: _____

_____

_____

Different styles of information text

 1 Read these short extracts from information texts. Who do you think the texts were written for? Write the letter of each extract below (A, B or C) in this table.

Viewpoint	Which text?
Written for much younger readers	
Written in a chatty, friendly style	
Written as an expert	

A To irrigate is to water crops by bringing in water from pipes, canals, sprinklers, or other manufactured means, rather than relying on rainfall alone.

B The Amazon rivers and forests are full of dazzling wildlife. Here, you can find the homes of thousands of plants and animals.

C Rivers often get their water from streams (smaller rivers) that join together. Imagine a child walking along a street. This child is joined by another and another to make a longer and wider line. This is similar to how some rivers grow.

 2 What is different about the language used in the children's text and the expert's viewpoint?

_____

 3 On a separate sheet of paper, rewrite this formal information text into a more child-friendly style. You should choose simpler words and write shorter sentences.

Amazon river dolphins have fat, **bulbous** foreheads and skinny, **elongated** beaks suited to snatching fish from a tangle of branches or to rooting around in river mud for **crustaceans**. They also have broad flippers, a reduced fin (a larger one would just get in the way in tight spots), and small eyes – **echolocation** helps them **pinpoint** prey in muddy water.

Glossary
bulbous: rounded (shaped like a bulb)
elongated: made longer than it is wide

crustaceans: shellfish
echolocation: the skill of finding directions by sending out a sound which echoes back
pinpoint: accurately find

4

The information in the table below is about the *Mary Celeste* ship, which was found in the Atlantic Ocean in 1872 with no people on board, and no damage or theft either. No one can explain what happened.

Use the language suggestions in the table below to write an information text as an expert. Choose suitable language from the table to use when you write your text.

Language to describe the boat	Language to describe where the boat was found	Language to describe who was on the boat	Language to describe what was left on the boat
• a boat • a merchant sailing vessel • a sailing ship	• discovered in the middle of the ocean • encountered drifting mid-ocean • found by another boat	• was deserted • there was no one on board • nobody was on the boat	• nothing was missing and the ship was not damaged • everything else was normal on the ship • the abandoned ship was still seaworthy (fine)

You could begin:

In 1872, a merchant sailing vessel known as … _____

_____

_____

_____

_____

_____

_____

_____

_____

_____

_____

_____

_____

_____

_____

_____

_____

Choosing how to lay out an information text

 1 Read the information below about the Mariana Trench, a deep underwater valley in the Pacific Ocean. Notice the different types of facts about this place.

The Mariana Trench is part of a global network of deep troughs that cut across the ocean floor. ⬭	In 1951, the British vessel HMS *Challenger II* returned to the spot with an echo-sounder and measured a depth of nearly 7 miles (11 kilometres). ⬭	It is located in the western Pacific east of the Philippines. ⬭
It is a crescent-shaped scar in the Earth's crust. ⬭	Only two people have descended to the planet's deepest point: Mariana Trench. ⬭	It is more than 1 500 miles (2 550 kilometres) long and 43 miles (69 kilometres) wide. ⬭
Thousands of climbers have successfully scaled Mount Everest, the highest point on the Earth. ⬭	If Mount Everest were dropped into the Mariana Trench, its peak would still be more than a mile (1.6 kilometres) underwater. ⬭	The depth was first measured (about 5 miles, or 8 kilometres) in 1875 by the British ship HMS *Challenger*, using a weighted rope. ⬭

 2 Divide the facts in the table above into four sub-headings, ready for writing an information text. Label each box in the table with a letter to show which sub-heading of the text it belongs to.

The Mariana Trench

A What is the Mariana Trench?
B Introduction
C How deep is the Mariana Trench?
D Where is the Mariana Trench?

What order would you put the sub-headings in? Write the letter to show the order.

 3 On a separate sheet of paper, plan how you want the information text to look on the page. Remember to show where you would like the title, the headings and the pictures to go. Add the sub-headings from question 2 to your plan to show where you want these sections to be placed.

Self-check

 I can do this.

 I can do this, but I need to keep trying.

 I can't do this yet.

What can I do?			
1 I can identify an information text and name the features used.			
2 I can explain the difference between an explanation text and an information text.			
3 I can recognise the viewpoint of an information text.			
4 I can skim and scan to find information.			
5 I can plan information texts, grouping facts into relevant sections.			
6 I can write information texts, choosing language to suit my readers.			
7 I can identify and use technical vocabulary.			
8 I can find alternatives to words that are overused or less precise.			
9 I can spell three words that end with the suffix **ology**.			
10 I can explain my opinion clearly.			

What do you need more help with? Write the number or numbers.

I need more help with:

_____

_____

Unit 5 — Fiction: Stories that have been developed into a film

The Invention of Hugo Cabret

1 This is a picture of an imaginary machine. Look carefully to identify the parts and add these labels to the drawing. An example has been done for you.

(cog) (teeth) (belt) (pipe) (clock face) (screws) (bolts) (tube) (key)

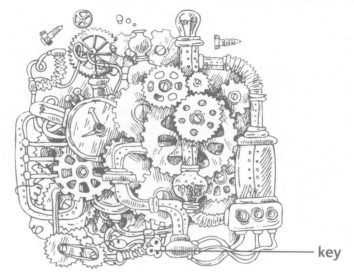

— key

2 These verbs can all be used to describe looking after this machine. On a separate sheet of paper, copy and complete the table below. Write the verb and then add your own ideas to the other two columns. An example has been done for you.

(wipe) (dust) (wash) (soak) (sterilise) (scour)

(brush) (scrape) (scrub) (mop) (disinfect)

Verbs that you could use to describe cleaning this machine	The equipment you would use to do this type of cleaning	Adverbs to show how you would perform this action
wipe	a cloth	gently, delicately

3 Imagine that Hugo had to care for this machine, as he does his clocks. Write a new paragraph for the story to describe how he does it. You could begin: *Hugo began his daily inspection of the magnificent machine …*

Use the words from question 2 to help you.

_____

_____

_____

_____

_____

Concrete and abstract nouns

 1 In this extract, Hugo tries to remember the pictures of the automaton and its workings that had been in his notebook (which the old man said he had burned).

Read carefully to notice all the feelings that Hugo experiences.

> Frustrated and sad and finished with the clocks, he finally returned to his room and tried to sleep. But his mind wouldn't stop spinning, and so he reached for a scrap of paper and a pencil from one of the boxes near his bed. He sat down on the floor and drew pictures of clocks and gears, imaginary machines and magicians on stage. He drew the automaton over and over and over again. He kept drawing as his mind calmed down. Then he slipped the drawings underneath his bed, onto the big pile of other drawings he had done, and climbed fully dressed into bed.

a Where did Hugo go after finishing his work? _____

b Why could he not sleep when he wanted to? _____

c Why was he drawing? _____

d What effect does drawing have on him? _____

 2 These abstract nouns could be used to name Hugo's thoughts and feelings in this extract.

On a separate sheet of paper, write each noun and copy the words in the text that support your choice. For example: *obsession: his mind wouldn't stop spinning*

a exhaustion

b distraction

c imagination

d anger

e quietness

f obsession

g tiredness

h concentration

Changing a story from a book to a film

 What do these sentences show you about Hugo's feelings? Complete the table.

Sentence	Explain what Hugo thinks or feels
Hugo's eyes lit up when he saw the automaton move.	
Hugo tightly clenched his fists.	
Hugo began to shiver so he rubbed his hands together.	

2 Read the adverbs below. Write a sentence using each adverb to describe something Hugo might do. For example: *Hugo might **silently** creep up the stairs to the clocks.*

a frantically _____

_____

b courageously _____

_____

c curiously _____

_____

d anxiously _____

_____

e joyfully _____

_____

Remember to record new words in your *Spelling log*.

 On a separate sheet of paper, write your own sentences, carefully choosing verbs and adverbs to show how Hugo feels. For example: *Hugo was tired.* → *Hugo yawned uncontrollably and his eyelids fluttered as he fought against sleep.*

a Hugo was hungry.

b Hugo was afraid.

c Hugo was happy.

Storyboards

 1 Read this extract. It describes Hugo completing his repair of the automaton and getting ready to wind it with the heart-shaped key.

Hugo had indeed been busy in the last week. He had finally repaired all of the mechanical man's broken pieces and painstakingly loosened what was too rusty to move. He had sewed it a new outfit, and oiled and polished its mechanisms. The mechanical man was finally holding a brand-new handmade pen with a specially cut metal nib.

Hugo moved a candle closer to him.

In the middle of the mechanical man's back was a heart-shaped hole, outlined in silver.

Since leaving the toy booth moments ago, Hugo's left hand had been clenched into a tight fist, which now he slowly opened like a flower.

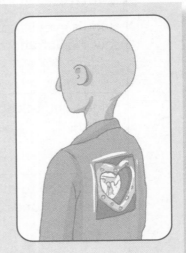

2 Think about how you could show this extract as a film. Divide the text into four sections, which will become four pictures for a storyboard. Use a pencil to mark your four sections on the extract.

3 To create the storyboard, choose the types of shot you will use (close-up, mid-shot or long shot) and make a sketch to show what a viewer would see on screen. Label each sketch with the camera angle you have used.

Using precise details in books and films

1 Read the extract. It describes what happened when Hugo was saved from being run over by the train. Look for the details that tell you what Hugo could see, hear and smell.

At the last possible moment, Hugo was yanked up, off the tracks, to safety. Smoke billowed out of the slowing engine as a shower of sparks flew from every wheel. Hugo felt dizzy.

There were a few moments of dazed silence, then steam was released from somewhere, and it made a sound like the train was sighing. For everyone on the train, nothing extraordinary had happened. They had simply pulled into the station. But for Hugo, his entire world was ending.

Again the Station Inspector was holding his arm, his injured hand throbbing with pain. He could see the policemen removing handcuffs from their belts, and finally the pain and the terror grew too much.

a On a separate sheet of paper, copy and complete this table using facts from the extract and information that can be inferred from the extract. Then answer questions b–e.

Hugo could see:	Hugo could hear:	Hugo could smell:

b How did the people on the train feel at this moment in the story?

c What is meant by Hugo's **entire world was ending**?

d What will the policemen do with Hugo?

e What is meant by **finally the pain and the terror grew too much**?

2 In the book *The Invention of Hugo Cabret*, the picture that follows the last sentence is just a blank box because the writer leaves us to imagine what could be going on in Hugo's mind. Imagine that Hugo fell into a dream. What would he see, hear, smell or taste in this dream?

a Complete this table to plan a paragraph. An example has been done for you.

What will Hugo see?	What will Hugo hear?	What will Hugo smell?	What will Hugo taste?
stars			
Precise words to describe these sensations			
twirling and twinkling in the midnight skies			

b On a separate sheet of paper, use your plan to write a paragraph to describe Hugo's dream. You could begin: *Hugo saw only blackness until a host of stars appeared, twirling and twinkling in the midnight skies …*

3 Circle the pronoun in each of the sentences below.

a Asim and Adam wrote a film review. Theirs was even better than the magazine's!

b 'Is the book yours?' asked Betty.

c The film makes some characters more important to the story than in the book because they are so interesting.

d We had to ask the girls to move and explain that the seats were ours.

4 Write the noun that each underlined pronoun refers to. An example has been done for you.

Jin and Maris were very happy to get tickets to see the film, *Hugo*, at the cinema. <u>They</u> had enjoyed reading the book and looked forward to seeing how it would appear on screen. '<u>I</u> hope <u>it</u> will be really imaginative,' Jin said.

'<u>I</u>'m sure <u>it</u> will be exciting as well,' said Maris. My friend has seen it already and <u>he</u> thought the special effects were excellent.

They – Jin and Maris

_____   _____

_____   _____

5 Complete each sentence with a different possessive pronoun of your choice.

a This is my bed and that is _____.

b Those books are _____.

c _____ is the second room

on the right.

d Is that T-shirt _____?

Check that you have used the correct form of the pronoun.

Self-check

 I can do this.

 I can do this, but I need to keep trying.

 I can't do this yet.

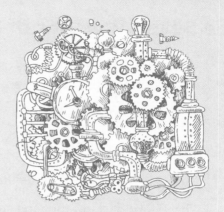

What can I do?			
1 I can scan a text to find precise information.			
2 I can identify abstract nouns that describe feelings and thoughts.			
3 I can select details from a story and present them in a storyboard.			
4 I can discuss how details may change from a book to a film.			
5 I can make predictions that show understanding of characters and of what might happen next in a story.			
6 I can create stories using carefully chosen words and phrases that help readers to see, hear and feel what is happening.			
7 I can plan and write sections of a story.			
8 I can choose adverbs to increase the impact of verbs.			
9 I can explain what a pronoun is.			
10 I can spell words with the **ie** spelling pattern.			
11 I can role-play scenes from the book to demonstrate understanding of characters.			

What do you need more help with? Write the number or numbers.

I need more help with:

_____

_____

The Seven Voyages of Sinbad the Sailor

1 Complete these sentences using an appropriate connective from the boxes below. Not all the connectives will be used.

(at that moment) (later) (meanwhile) (until) (where) (wherever) (so)

(therefore) (consequently) (as a result) (since)

a _____ of being pulled away by the sea's currents, Sinbad lost his companions.

b Sinbad found that the sand was coarse and unfamiliar, _____ he knew this was a land he had not seen before and _____ he felt very alone.

c The horse, which had a saddle but no rider, kicked _____ it was too tired to kick anymore.

d _____ his crew did not recognise him, Sinbad tried to make them believe he was who he said he was.

e Sinbad lost his possessions _____ he went, but he became wealthier than before when he arrived home.

f Sinbad loved to travel. _____, he would not stay at home for long.

2 Complete the sentences using appropriate connectives from the boxes below.

(luckily) (unluckily) (fortunately) (unfortunately) (sadly)

(nevertheless) (on the other hand) (in spite of) (although)

(also) (moreover) (in addition) (however) (as well as)

(**a**) _____ Sinbad experienced a series of problems, he wanted to travel. He loved to travel (**b**) _____ all the risks and danger.
(**c**) _____, Sinbad never really came to any real harm. He got into many dangerous situations, (**d**) _____. (**e**) _____ meeting danger, Sinbad (**f**) _____ met a lot of strange creatures on his journeys.
(**g**) _____ he managed to survive!

3 Work with a partner. Choose five of the connectives not used in question 2 and list them below. Write sentences using these connectives on a separate sheet of paper.

_____

_____

_____

_____

The second voyage

1 Complete the table to show which figurative language is used in each sentence: simile, metaphor, personification or a combination of these. An example has been done for you.

Sentence		Simile	Metaphor	Personification
a	The serpents in the cave were ribbons of destruction writhing about Sinbad's ankles.		✓	
b	The teeth gleamed like cold, steel knives about to cut steak.			
c	The ground rushed to meet us as we landed.			
d	I felt like a rocket flying to the stars above.			
e	The wind whispered around my head, but I walked on.			
f	The eyes were two red hot coals burning through the darkness.			

2 Use adverbs to emphasise the adjectives used to describe the roc's features. You can choose from the boxes below or use your own choices. An example has been done for you.

(deeply) (carefully) (painfully) (completely) (highly)

a   <u>completely</u>   outstretched wings

b   _____ threatening claws

c   _____ sharpened beak

d   _____ shrill cries

e   _____ piercing eyes

3 Write a paragraph to describe the actions in the picture in question 2. Use a range of figurative language such as alliteration, simile, metaphor and adverb–adjective combinations.

You could begin: _The roc descended like a …_ _____

_____

_____

_____

_____

The third voyage

 1 On a separate sheet of paper, write labels for this picture using adjectives to describe what the giant looks like, for example:

- *awe-inspiring*
- *muscular*
- *towering*
- *immense.*

 2 On a separate sheet of paper, write a description to show the giant's strength.

a Make a list of powerful verbs in the past tense to show his strength when he uprooted and threw the tree, for example: *hurled, tossed, heaved.*

b Add an adverb to each of the verbs, for example: ***furiously** hurled.*

c Write your description on a separate sheet of paper. You could begin: *The immense creature raised a mighty fist and …*

 3 Read this extract, which tells what happened to the giant after Sinbad bound him. Again, think about how Sinbad feels about the giant.

> The pit wasn't deep but with his arms and feet tied he couldn't climb back out. Instead he rolled around **pitifully** as the fire consumed him. The other men cheered but I couldn't help feeling sad. The giant hadn't been cruel to us on purpose, he was **merely** feeding himself.

> **Glossary**
> **pitifully**: helplessly
> **merely**: just, only

a How does the writer show that the giant is helpless?

_____

b Which word does Sinbad use to show sympathy for the giant?

_____

c Why does Sinbad have some sympathy for the giant?

_____

 4 Sinbad's viewpoint about the giant changes from one of fear to one of sympathy when the giant is suffering.

On a separate sheet of paper, draw a sketch to show the giant crying. Label your sketch with verbs to show what the giant is doing, for example: *weep, wail, sob, whimper.*

> Use a thesaurus to help you find more words for **cry**. Make a list of adjectives to describe the giant that will show some sympathy for it, such as *poor, helpless, weakened* and *isolated.*

 5 On a separate sheet of paper, write a description of the giant crying and show that Sinbad is sympathetic to the giant.

The fourth voyage

 1 Read this extract in which Sinbad is again lost at sea. Notice the underlined words and think about what they mean.

After two or three days floating <u>aimlessly</u>, I <u>perceived</u> a ship and <u>rapidly</u> I untied my red turban to wave like a flag. Luck was with me and they sent a rowboat to bring me on board. When the captain saw my ragged clothes and even more ragged beard he was <u>unwilling</u> to take me on board, until I offered him a handful of pearls from the rope I had made. This <u>motley</u> crew was not to be trusted though, and I hid the rest of the pearls very carefully. I <u>disembarked</u> at the first port we landed in and hurried to sell my pearls to make enough money to pay for passage home on a better ship.

a For how long was Sinbad in the sea?

b What was he wearing and how did it help him?

c Why was the captain suspicious of Sinbad?

d What precious jewels did Sinbad have?

e What did he think the crew might do?

Answer questions **a–e** on a separate sheet of paper.

2 Look at the underlined words in the extract above and work out their meanings to complete the table below. Check your answers using a dictionary. An example has been done for you.

Remember to record new words in your *Spelling log*.

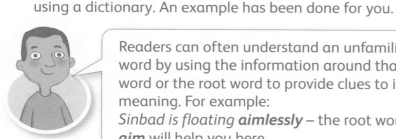

Readers can often understand an unfamiliar word by using the information around that word or the root word to provide clues to its meaning. For example:
Sinbad is floating **aimlessly** – the root word **aim** will help you here.

Word in the extract	What I think it means	Check the definition in a dictionary. Were you correct?
aimlessly	without aim – no direction	✓
perceived		
rapidly		
unwilling		
motley		
disembarked		

The fifth voyage

 1 Copy the table below onto a separate sheet of paper. Write these verbs used to report speech into three groups in the table. Some examples have been done for you.

(say) (roar) (hiss) (reply) (whisper) (describe) (mutter) (show) (scream)

(demonstrate) (compliment) (note) (snap) (grumble) (growl) (yell)

(report) (congratulate) (mention) (splutter) (comment) (praise) (observe)

Verbs that describe how loudly someone is speaking	Verbs that show an emotion	Neutral verbs that do not show an emotion
mutter	congratulate	reply

 2 **a** Add the correct punctuation to this conversation between Sinbad and the Old Man of the Sea. Use capital letters, speech marks, commas, question marks and full stops. An example has been done for you.

W

'~~w~~hat have you done to me **said** the old man

of the sea when he awoke you have done this

to yourself **said** Sinbad with your bad treatment

of me release me immediately he **said** of course

I won't Sinbad **said** you would just trick me again

b On a separate sheet of paper, rewrite the text correctly. Change the word **said** in the conversation for more precise verbs to report speech. Use the verbs in the table in question 1 to help you.

3 Imagine that you have arrived at the island in the story and you find the Old Man of the Sea in the pit. On a separate sheet of paper, write a dialogue between yourself and the Old Man of the Sea.

Remember to vary your verbs to report speech. You could begin: *'What on earth are you doing down there?'* I enquired.

The sixth voyage

1 Read these extracts about Sinbad's journey along the river. Look at the underlined adverbs and adverbial phrases in each extract. Notice how the writer uses a variety of adverbs and adverbial phrases to add detail.

In the dark the wall did come against my head and knocked me clean out. It was lucky I had tied myself to the raft for safety otherwise I surely would have fallen off and drowned. When I awoke I was no longer in the cave. Instead I was merrily floating upriver, through lush fields of farmed crops. It was quiet and peaceful, and I felt very grateful to be alive still. After a while I began to gather the attention of some local people; this enchanted island was inhabited after all.

I waved in a friendly manner and together we got my raft to the bank so I could climb out. Having met locals before who ended up less than nice despite their **perceived hospitality**, I was a little nervous; but the thought of solid ground after my **turmoil-filled** journey was too inviting.

perceived hospitality: they seemed welcoming (but Sinbad couldn't be sure)
turmoil-filled: filled with difficulties

a How did Sinbad get knocked out?

b Why did he not drown?

c How did he feel when he woke up?

d Who did he see?

e Why was he worried about getting off the raft?

f Why did he get off the raft?

Answer questions **a–f** on a separate sheet of paper.

2 The writer has used adverbs and adverbial phrases to increase the level of detail in the extracts. On a separate sheet of paper, change the underlined adverbs and adverbial phrases in the extract to synonyms. For example: *In the dark – In the inky blackness*

a knocked me **clean out**

b I **surely** would have fallen off

c I was **merrily** floating upriver

d I waved **in a friendly manner**

e Having met locals before who ended up less than nice **despite their perceived hospitality**

f but the thought of solid ground **after my turmoil-filled journey**

47

The seventh voyage

1 Correctly add these words to the passage below to create a description of classic literature.

(time)   (long ago)   (bravery)   (modern)   (stories)   **(duty)**

(imagination)   (themes)   (thoughts)   (honour)

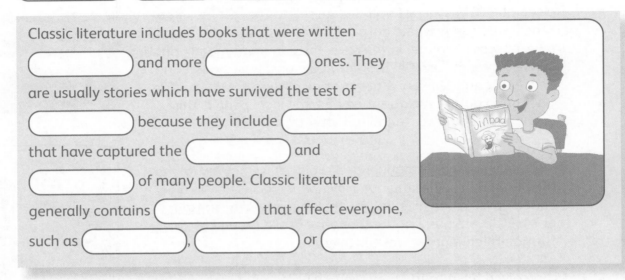

Classic literature includes books that were written

(   ) and more (   ) ones. They

are usually stories which have survived the test of

(   ) because they include (   )

that have captured the (   ) and

(   ) of many people. Classic literature

generally contains (   ) that affect everyone,

such as (   ), (   ) or (   ).

2 The themes below are found in *The Seven Voyages of Sinbad the Sailor.* Give an example of how each theme is shown in the story. An example has been done for you.

Glossary
duty: having a responsibility to do something
equality: all people being treated the same
greed: selfishly wanting something
courage: being brave

a **equality** – *Even though the porter is poor, Sinbad treats him with the same respect as he would a rich man.*

b friendship

c honour

d kindness to animals

e **greed**

f selfishness

g **courage**

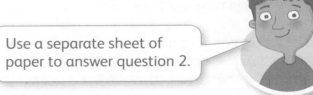

Use a separate sheet of paper to answer question 2.

3 Which is your favourite adventure in *The Seven Voyages of Sinbad the Sailor*? On a separate sheet of paper, write a paragraph to explain why you like this adventure best. Include:
- a description of the adventure
- the theme of the adventure
- what you particularly like about it.

Self-check

 I can do this.

 I can do this, but I need to keep trying.

 I can't do this yet.

What can I do?			
1 I can give two reasons why a story might be called a 'classic'.			
2 I can comment on how a reader today and a reader in the past may think about a story differently.			
3 I can identify a theme in a story and explain my opinion about it.			
4 I can find out the meaning of unfamiliar words by using clues in the text.			
5 I can create interesting compound sentences using connectives.			
6 I can use adverbs and adverbial phrases to add detail and interest to my sentences.			
7 I can recognise and create a simile, a metaphor and an example of personification.			
8 I can accurately use commas to separate parts of sentences.			
9 I can add dialogue to a story and punctuate it correctly.			
10 I can recognise and explain the meanings of some homonyms.			
11 I can identify a modal verb.			
12 I can discuss my ideas with a partner and in a small group.			

What do you need more help with? Write the number or numbers.

I need more help with:

_____

_____

Playscripts: A playscript, book and film of the same story

Comparing playscripts and books

1 Roald Dahl wrote many books for children, and some of these have been turned into plays and films. Match the names of the features of playscripts with the play examples below. Write a letter in each box.

A scene title **B** stage directions **C** roles
D lines **E** title of the play

Charlie and the Chocolate Factory ☐

Scene 1 ☐

NARRATOR: *[Enters in front of curtain.]* Welcome to the tale of a delicious adventure in a wonderful land. You can tell it will be delicious – can't you smell it already? ☐ *[Sniffs]* ☐

Characters ☐
(in order of appearance)
Narrator
Augustus Gloop
Veruca Salt
…

2 Read the extracts below from *Charlie and the Chocolate Factory*, a book and play by Roald Dahl. The story is about a young boy called Charlie who lives near a very special chocolate factory.

BOOK

Twice a day, on his way to and from school, little Charlie Bucket had to walk right past the gates of the factory. And every time he went by, he would begin to walk very, very slowly, and he would hold his nose high in the air and take long deep sniffs of the gorgeous chocolatey smell all around him.

Oh how he loved that smell.

PLAY

CHARLIE: You know … it just about makes me faint when I have to pass Mr Wonka's Chocolate Factory every day as I go to school. The smell of that wonderful chocolate makes me so dreamy that I often fall asleep and bump into Mr Wonka's fence.

What is similar and different about the book and play extracts? Copy and complete this table on a separate sheet of paper.

	Book	Play
When does Charlie pass the factory?		
What does the smell make him do?		
What words are used to describe the chocolate smell?		

3 Write this sentence from the book as a line in the play.
Oh how he loved that smell. _____

Stagecraft

1 Read this extract from the play *James and the Giant Peach*, Scene 3. The Narrator is describing what the giant peach is doing – but this can't be seen by the audience. Think about how the Narrator should sound and what he or she should do while delivering this speech.

> NARRATOR: I wonder what that noise was? Well, anyway, you'll never believe it, but the Giant Peach is still moving. It's rolling and bouncing down the steep slope at a terrific pace. It's going faster and faster and faster, and the crowds of people who were climbing up the hill have suddenly caught sight of it plunging down upon them. They're screaming and scattering to the right and left. It's just knocked over a telegraph pole and flattened two parked cars.

a   Where is the giant peach going? _____

_____

b   Which words tell you how fast it is going? _____

_____

c   What do the people do when the giant peach approaches? _____

_____

d   What damage does the giant peach cause? _____

_____

2 Write stage directions for the Narrator to deliver this speech in a dynamic and engaging way, rather than just saying the lines. An example has been done for you.

Lines from script	How the Narrator should sound and what he or she should do
I wonder what that noise was?	*[Sounding concerned and looking to all sides and up and down.]*
It's going faster and faster and faster.	
They're screaming and scattering to the right and left.	
It's just knocked over a telegraph pole and flattened two parked cars.	

3 Look back at the playscript extract on page 51. How might these events look in a film? Draw a picture in each of the frames below. Add speech bubbles to show what the people would say.

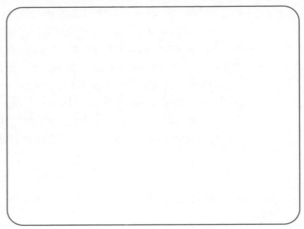

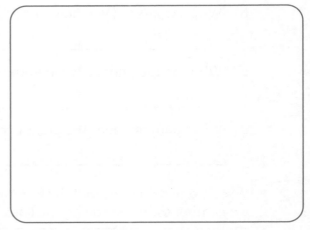

4 Rewrite these sentences correctly, adding possessive apostrophes.

a The peachs skin was not even bruised by the bounces.

b As the peach passed, a childs hat was blown off.

c A telegraph poles wires became tangled up.

d Two parked cars windows were smashed.

_____

_____

_____

_____

Characters

1 This extract is from the book *James and the Giant Peach* by Roald Dahl. The creatures and James are surrounded by hungry sharks and they need a plan to escape them. Read the extract and think about how the characters respond to the crisis.

'There *is* something that I believe we might try,' James Henry Trotter said slowly. 'I'm not saying it'll work …'

'Tell us!' cried the Earthworm 'Tell us quick!'

'We'll try anything you say!' said the Centipede. 'But hurry, hurry, hurry!'

'Be quiet and let the boy speak!' said the Ladybird. 'Go on, James.'

They all moved a little closer to him. There was a longish pause.

'Go on!' they cried frantically. *'Go on!'*

And all the time while they were waiting, they could hear the sharks **threshing** around in the water below them. It was enough to make anyone frantic.

Glossary

threshing: moving about and making the water churn up

2 Answer these questions about the extract on a separate sheet of paper.

a What does James mean when he says, 'There *is* something that I believe we might try'?

b Why does Centipede say, 'We'll try anything'?

c Why does Ladybird tell the others to be quiet?

d What do you think **frantically** means in this extract?

e What were the sharks hoping to do?

3 On a separate sheet of paper, complete the table using the adjectives in the boxes below to describe how the characters behave in the extract in question 1. An example has been done for you.

(inventive) (doubtful) (impatient) (calming) (panicky) (reassuring)

(convinced) (optimistic) (encouraging) (hopeful) (hesitant) (apologetic)

James	Ladybird	Earthworm	Centipede
inventive			

4 Complete the sentences with an appropriate comparative or superlative form. Remember these are all irregular adjectives and adverbs.

a Is your headache still _____? Yes, it's _____ than yesterday. It's _____ it's ever been!

b The last series was _____, but this year's is even _____. You have to watch it!

c This is _____ film I've ever seen. It is amazing!

d There are _____ plays being made because they are rather expensive to make.

e The film did _____ than expected. It wasn't popular at the box office.

f The book went a lot _____ into the characters than the film did. I preferred the book.

g Everyone seems to have _____ time to read these days. It's a real shame.

h He said that all of those horror books were scary, but this one is _____ scary. So I think I'll try reading that one. I do get scared quite easily!

5 Rewrite the book extract on page 53 as a playscript. You could begin:

JAMES: *[Thoughtfully]* There *is* something that I believe we might try …

> Use a separate sheet of paper.

6 Copy the matching synonym from the boxes for each of the words below.

(comrades) (damage) (voyage) (creatures) (difficulty) (scheme)

a challenge _____   b plan _____

c journey _____   d friends _____

e insects _____   f destruction _____

7 Rewrite the sentence below, replacing each underlined word with its antonym.

The peach was <u>enormous</u> and when it rolled <u>rapidly</u> down the hill, it destroyed <u>everything</u> in its path.

> **Remember:** A synonym is a word that means exactly or nearly exactly the same as another word.
> An antonym is a word with the opposite meaning. For example: *good – **bad**.*

_____

_____

_____

_____

Reported speech

1 Choose a suitable verb from the boxes to complete the sentences containing reported speech. Some verbs may be used more than once, while others may not be used at all.

(boasted) (bragged) (clucked) (giggled) (grumbled) (jabbered)

(moaned) (ranted) (revealed) (scolded) (squawked) (urged) (yelled)

a Earthworm _____ that he would be the first to be eaten.

b Centipede _____ that his shoes were always clean.

c They all _____ that James should find a solution to the problem.

d Earthworm _____ that he needed to hide inside the giant peach.

e Spider _____ that she could spin beautiful threads.

2 Change these sentences from direct speech into reported speech. Use a separate sheet of paper.

a Earthworm: I don't like this at all.

b Spider: Do you think they can see us?

c James: It's working!

d Officer: Do you think it's following us?

e Captain: I don't like it!

3 Change the passage of reported speech between James and Ladybird, from the book *James and the Giant Peach,* into a script for the play or the film.

James said he now thought he knew what to do. Ladybird immediately asked him what his plan was, but James replied that he didn't have a plan yet. Ladybird told him not to worry and that he would think of one very soon.

_____

_____

_____

_____

_____

_____

_____

Characters and viewpoints

1 Read this extract from the book *James and the Giant Peach*. Earthworm is explaining to James how people view earthworms.

'You mean you actually *swallow* soil?'

'Like mad,' the Earthworm said proudly. '*In* one end and *out* the other.'

'But what's the point?'

'What do you mean, what's the point?'

'Why do you do it?'

'We do it for the farmers. It makes the soil nice and light and crumbly so that things will grow well in it.'

a Why is James surprised?

b Why is Earthworm proud?

c Why do farmers love earthworms?

Answer questions **a–e** on a separate sheet of paper.

d When James asks: 'You mean you actually *swallow* soil?', why is *swallow* in italics? What is James' opinion about Earthworm swallowing soil?

e Earthworm asks James: 'What do you mean, what's the point?' What is Earthworm's opinion of James?

2 Read this extract about how people view spiders and answer the questions below.

But what about you, Miss Spider?' asked James. 'Aren't you also much loved in the world?'

'Alas, no,' Miss Spider answered, sighing long and loud. 'I am not loved at all. And yet I do nothing but good. All day long I catch flies and mosquitoes in my webs. I am a decent person.'

'I know you are,' said James.

a Why did Miss Spider sigh?

b What good things does she say that spiders do?

c What is James' viewpoint about Miss Spider? Underline the phrases in the text that show you this.

d What is Miss Spider's viewpoint about herself? Circle the phrases in the text that show you this.

Answer questions **a–d** on a separate sheet of paper.

3 Write a response to Miss Spider from James' viewpoint.
What could he say to cheer her up?

_____

_____

_____

_____

4 Look back at Miss Spider's words in the extract on page 56. Imagine making a film of this moment and wanting to show how decent spiders are. What images would you use? Draw two frames to show this viewpoint.

5 Imagine that you want to show a negative viewpoint of Miss Spider at this moment in the film. You want to make her seem scary and unpleasant. What images would you use? Draw two frames on a separate sheet of paper to show this viewpoint.

> Think about how Miss Spider could look, speak and behave as she talks to James. How would this affect James' opinion of her?

6 Complete this paragraph about viewpoints using the words in boxes. Write one word in each box in the paragraph below.

(different) (same) (positive) (negative) (suggest) (think)

The (_____) events can be seen from (_____) viewpoints. In a film, how a character looks, speaks and behaves can help to (_____) a viewpoint. In books, writers' choice of words will show whether they want you to (_____) of a character in a (_____) or (_____) way.

Working as a group

 Imagine that your class is going to perform the play *James and the Giant Peach*.

Decide which roles would best suit the people in your class, giving a positive reason why you have chosen that person.

Role	Name	Why I chose this person
Director (the person who organises everyone)		
Narrator		
James		
Ladybird		
Centipede		
Earthworm		
Old-Green-Grasshopper		
Miss Spider		
Cloud-Men		
Sharks		

2 From your experiences of working as a group to perform scenes from *James and the Giant Peach*, write two instructions to help people to work successfully with others. For example: *One person should speak at a time – not all at once.*

_____

_____

_____

_____

Spelling unstressed vowel phonemes

1 **a** Work out the clues and write the correct spelling of these words with unstressed vowels. An example has been done for you.

To show that something is needed.   <u>necessary</u>

Something that is not joined to another thing.   s_____

To think of something from the past.   r_____

Not the same as anything else.   d_____

b Write a sentence about the story of *James and the Giant Peach* using each of the unstressed words in question 1.

_____

_____

_____

_____

2 Underline the words with unstressed vowels in the extract below.

Even though there were lots of interesting things to see on their adventures, the creatures were often frightened. However, James was the steady centre of their world and could generally find a solution to the problems they faced. They became James' new family as they all cared for each other.

3 Write a paragraph to describe what happened at the end of the film, play or book, including as many of these words with unstressed vowels as possible.

(intelligent) (similar) (medicine) (original) (officer) (helicopter)

_____

_____

_____

_____

_____

_____

Self-check

 I can do this.

 I can do this, but I need to keep trying.

 I can't do this yet.

What can I do?			
1 I can identify features of a playscript.			
2 I can notice similarities and differences between a book, a playscript and a film of the same story.			
3 I can read with expression.			
4 I can use gestures, facial expressions and frozen moments to show characters and events.			
5 I can understand the personalities of characters from what they say.			
6 I can create scenes for a script of my own.			
7 I can use stage directions to show how a script should be performed.			
8 I can identify synonyms and antonyms.			
9 I can spell words with unstressed vowel phonemes.			
10 I can write sentences using direct speech and reported speech.			
11 I can correctly use apostrophes.			
12 I can choose the correct pronoun to replace a noun.			
13 I can work successfully within a group.			

What do you need more help with? Write the number or numbers.

I need more help with:

_____

_____

Unit 8   Poetry: Poems by famous poets

Simple poems with powerful messages

1 Read this poem by African American poet, Langston Hughes (1902–1967). He wrote poetry from an early age but became famous when working as a **bus boy**, when he left three of his poems on the table beside an already famous poet. The next day, all the city newspapers were talking about Langston.

In this poem, a mother explains to her son that life is going to be hard.

Mother to Son

Well, son, I'll tell you:
Life for me ain't been no **crystal** stair.
It's had **tacks** in it,
And splinters,
And boards torn up,
And places with no carpet on the floor— Bare.
But all the time
I'se been **a-climbin'** on,
And **reachin' landin's**,
And **turnin'** corners,
And sometimes **goin'** in the dark
Where there **ain't** been no light.
So, boy, don't you turn back.
Don't you **set down** on the steps.
'Cause you finds it's **kinder hard**.
Don't you fall now—
For I'se still goin', **honey**,
I'se still climbin',
And life for me ain't been no crystal stair.

By Langston Hughes

Glossary	
bus boy: a general assistant in a hotel or restaurant	**turnin'**: turning
	goin': going
crystal: glass	**ain't**: has not
tacks: nails	**set down**: sit down
I'se: I've	**'cause**: because
a-climbing: climbing	**kinder hard**: kind of hard
reachin': reaching	**honey**: an endearment like 'dear' or 'darling'
landin's: landings	

2 On a separate sheet of paper, answer these questions about the meanings in the poem.

a The mother represents the problems in life with problems on the stairs. She describes them as **places with no carpet on the floor**.
Find two other phrases used to represent life's problems.

b Find two verbs that tell you that the mother has spent her life trying to get away from the problems of life, for example: *climbin'*.

c What advice does the mother give to her son?

d What does the mother mean by a **crystal stair**?

3 Circle the correct word or words in brackets to complete this sentence:
The poet uses apostrophes to make the words sound like (non-standard English / formal language / poetic language).

Exploring figurative language

 Underline the word in each sentence that makes the sentence an example of personification.

a The wind whispered through the dry grass.

b The fire swallowed the entire forest.

c Flags danced in the breeze.

d The sun smiled down on us.

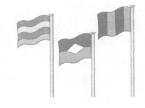

e The alarm clock screamed at me to get up.

f The streetlights winked in the darkness.

g The flowers were begging for water.

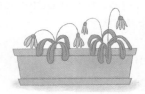

 On a separate sheet of paper, match the two parts of these examples of personification. Write your answers like this, for example: *e – The creeper wove its fingers tightly **around the tree***.

a	Lightning did spectacular gymnastics	the mountain trails.
b	The cutting wind prowled	around the tree.
c	The sofa complained	calling my name.
d	The last piece of pizza was	across the sky.
e	The creeper wove its fingers tightly	as Aunt Millicent sat down.

 Write your own examples of personification for the objects you can see in this picture.

a The houses _____

_____

_____

b The chimneys _____

_____

_____

c The boats _____

d The trees _____

e The clouds _____

f The river _____

Exploring meaning in a classic poem

1 This classic poem was written by the English poet Alfred, Lord Tennyson in 1832. These verses are from a longer narrative poem that tells the story of the Lady of Shalott, who lives in the castle of Camelot. She is forbidden to look directly out of the window so she must look at life outside in the reflection in a mirror.

Verse 1

On either side the river lie
Long fields of **barley** and of **rye**,
That **clothe** the **wold** and meet the sky;
And **thro'** the field the road runs by
    To many-**tower'd Camelot**;
The yellow-leaved **waterlily**
The green-sheathed **daffodilly**
Tremble in the water chilly
    Round about **Shalott**.

Glossary

barley: a crop, like wheat

rye: a crop, like wheat

clothe: covers

wold: moor land

thro': through

tower'd: towered

Camelot: the name of a castle

waterlily: a type of water flower

daffodilly: Daffodil (type of flower)

Shalott: the name of an island

List the places and objects that appear in Verse 1 of the poem, for example: *river, barley*.

_____

_____

2 Now read the next verse of the poem and answer the questions below.

Verse 2

No time **hath** she to sport and play:
A charmed **web** she weaves always.
A curse is on her, if she **stay**
Her weaving, either night or day,
    To look down to Camelot.
She knows not what the curse may be;
Therefore she **weaveth steadily**,
Therefore no other care hath she,
    The Lady of Shalott.

Glossary

hath: has

web: the cloth she is weaving

stay: stop

weaveth: weaves

steadily: all the time

a Are each of these statements true or false? Tick **T** for 'true' or **F** for 'false'.

The Lady only weaves at night.   T ☐   F ☐

She will die if she looks down on Camelot.   T ☐   F ☐

She likes being in her room.   T ☐   F ☐

b What language makes this poem sound old-fashioned or historical?

_____

_____

Exploring mood

  1 Read the next verse of the poem, which continues the story of the Lady of Shalott. She has looked down from her window so that she can clearly see a handsome knight who is riding past on his horse. Notice how the mood has changed from the verses on page 63.

> **Verse 3**
>
> She left the **web**, she left the loom
> She made three paces **thro'** the room
> She saw the waterlily bloom,
> She saw the helmet and the **plume**,
>   She look'd down to Camelot.
> Out flew the web and floated wide;
> The mirror crack'd from side to side;
> 'The curse is come upon me,' cried
>   The Lady of Shalott.

> **Glossary**
> **web**: the cloth she is weaving
> **thro'**: across or through the room
> **plume**: decorative feathers in a helmet

a What real things did the Lady of Shalott see when she looked out of her window?

b What happened to the cloth she was weaving?

c What happened to the mirror?

d What did the Lady say?

> Answer questions **a–d** on a separate sheet of paper.

2 **a** What kind of mood has the poet created in this verse? Explain why you think this.

_____

_____

_____

b Look back at page 63. What kinds of mood are created in Verse 1 and Verse 2. Choose from these words. Explain why you think this.

(peaceful)   (pleasant)   (mysterious)   (dangerous)   (tragic)

Verse
1
2

3 What do you think will happen to the Lady now? On a separate sheet of paper, write four lines to continue the poem.

Words that do not follow rules

1 Find and write the meanings of these common exception words using a dictionary. Practise spelling the words using the Look – Say – Cover – Write – Check method.

a anxious _____

b vicious _____

c protein _____

d seize _____

e argument _____

f truly _____

g wholly _____

h attention _____

i intention _____

j yacht _____

2 Create mnemonics for the words below.

Mnemonics (ni-**mon**-iks) are imaginative clues to help you to remember spellings. For example: **necessary**: **n**ever **e**at **c**ucumber; **e**at **s**imple **s**andwiches **a**nd **r**emain **y**oung.

a surprise _____

b though _____

c because _____

3 a Match the pairs of words below that have the same meaning. They are examples of English spoken in different countries. An example has been done for you.

bill	elevator
sweets	smart
chips	faucet
tap	mad
lift	check
clever	candy
angry	fries

b Write sentences using as many pairs of words above as you can. Continue on a separate sheet of paper if you run out of space.

_____

_____

_____

Unit 8 Poetry: Poems by famous poets

Self-check

 I can do this.

 I can do this, but I need to keep trying.

 I can't do this yet.

What can I do?	😉	😐	🙁
1 I can read poems aloud with confidence.			
2 I can present poems using drama.			
3 I can understand personification and create my own examples.			
4 I can identify words that are standard English and some that are not.			
5 I can design the layout of a poem in two different ways.			
6 I can create poems using simple language, simile and metaphor.			
7 I can explain whether the mood of a poem is positive or negative.			
8 I can give three examples of homonyms.			
9 I can explain how I choose to learn the spellings of common exception words.			

What do you need more help with? Write the number or numbers.

I need more help with:

_____

_____

Unit 9 — Non-fiction: Persuasive texts

Features of persuasive texts

1 Read the letter and answer the questions below.

Dear Reader,

Do you need to drive that car to school today? Could you have walked the short distance from your house to your school? Could you be a walking wonder, a change-maker to improve our world?

You probably know that traffic fumes are a major cause of pollution, particularly in large towns and cities.

Pollution in the air creates dangerous health problems such as **asthma** (which means that people find it difficult to breathe normally). Studies show that asthma has rapidly increased because the number of cars on the road has risen. Take one step in the right direction and you can change the world! Let's work together to make life better for children with this condition – not worse.

With so many cars on the road, **congestion** in towns and cities means that travel by car might not be much quicker than on foot or on a bicycle. The average speed of traffic in our cities is now only 12 miles (19 km) per hour, the same as it was 100 years ago when people were just using animals and bicycles for transport!

> **Glossary**
> **asthma:** an illness that makes breathing difficult
> **congestion:** crowded with traffic, making it difficult to move

a What does this persuasive letter want people to do? Tick one box.

- Drive smaller cars. ☐
- Ban cars from cities. ☐
- Raise money to prevent asthma. ☐
- Walk to school. ☐

b Find and copy an example of:

- a rhetorical question. _____
- alliteration. _____
- a powerful adjective. _____
- exaggeration. _____

c What two problems with traffic does the letter mention?

_____

d What can the reader of the letter do to help solve these problems?

_____

_____

Using facts and opinions to persuade

1 Read the passage below. Write three facts and three opinions about the car.

I've got a brand-new convertible car. It's the most incredible car in the world. I saved up a lot of money to buy it. It is bright green and absolutely fantastic to drive! It goes very fast and makes me look very cool. People will be really impressed by it.

_____

_____

_____

_____

_____

_____

2 What viewpoint is shown in the statements below? Write the correct letter in each box.

(calm and logical [   ])   (emotional [   ])   (argumentative [   ])

A Social media is destroying children's cherished childhoods and causing mental health catastrophes.

B Even though social media is easy to access, that doesn't mean that children should be using it so frequently.

C What would the world be without social media? Who wants to send us back into a world where communication is outside individual control?

3 Write a paragraph to persuade your teacher to allow you to use mobile phones (cell phones) for tasks in the classroom. Include facts and opinions.

_____

_____

_____

_____

_____

_____

Organising a persuasive text

 Imagine that your school has been given a large sum of money to donate to a charity.

Choose a charity that you would like your classmates to support. Use the table below to plan a speech to persuade them.

Do some research and find three reasons to support your charity. Put the reasons in order, saving the strongest reason until last. Then complete this table. Continue on a separate sheet of paper if you run out of space.

Paragraph	Name of charity:	
1	Introduction – which charity I am supporting and why	
2	Least important reason for supporting my charity	
	Supporting evidence or example	
3	Medium important reason for supporting my charity	
	Supporting evidence or example	
4	Most important reason for supporting my charity	
	Supporting evidence or example	
5	Conclusion – sum up my reasons and remind the audience which charity I am supporting	

More methods of persuasion

  One method of persuading people to take action is to show them how their world could be much better. A description of a **perfect** world can help to persuade.

Writers create this world by choosing words to make the imaginary scene come alive. On a separate sheet of paper, copy and complete the table below by creating persuasive sentences to describe an ideal world. You could use these phrases to begin your sentences:

(Imagine …)   (How proud would you be …)   (Build a new future …)

An example has been done for you.

	How money could be used	Sentences to persuade
Children's charity	Help children to go to school	Imagine a classroom full of smiling faces, eager for education and a better future.
Animal charity	Help to protect rhinos from poachers	Build a new future where …
Charity to help homeless people	Provide a night in a shelter with hot food	
Charity to help elderly people	Invite lonely people to a weekly lunch	
Animal charity	Give veterinary care to abandoned pets	

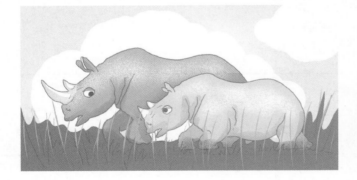 

2 Go back to your plan on page 69. Write a sentence for each of paragraphs 2, 3 and 4 that will show how the world will be better if your chosen charity is supported.

_____

_____

_____

_____

_____

_____

Persuading a chosen audience

 1 Using the plan on page 69 and the persuasive sentence starters on page 70 and below, write a speech to persuade your classmates to support the charity of your choice. Choose language and methods of persuasion that will work for this audience. For example, you may think an informal approach is more appropriate than a formal one.

- **Rhetorical questions** – *Do you want to make a difference?*
- **Exaggeration** – *Your efforts can change everything.*
- **Powerful adjectives** – (*appreciative animals*) and **verbs** (*act now*)
- **Comments** from people who want your help.
- **Alliteration** – *Your cash can create comfort …*
- **Imperative verbs** – *Donate now, don't delay!*

Write your speech here:

_____

_____

_____

_____

_____

_____

_____

_____

_____

_____

_____

_____

_____

_____

_____

_____

_____

_____

_____

Unit 9 Non-fiction: Persuasive texts

Self-check

 I can do this.

 I can do this, but I need to keep trying.

 I can't do this yet.

What can I do?			
1 I can recognise persuasion in texts such as letters and commentaries.			
2 I can identify persuasive features and persuasive language.			
3 I can identify facts and opinions, and how they are used to persuade.			
4 I can recognise the viewpoint of the writer in a persuasive text.			
5 I can find and use synonyms for persuasive effects.			
6 I can explain how pictures help to persuade.			
7 I can create rhetorical questions and write descriptions of 'ideal' images that persuade.			
8 I can choose a formal or informal tone to persuade a particular audience.			
9 I can use adverbs and adverbial phrases to add precise information to persuasive texts.			
10 I can plan and write a complete persuasive text of my own.			
11 I can read persuasive texts with expression to have an impact on listeners.			
12 I can discuss ideas with others, taking a role in the presentation of an advert.			

 What do you need more help with? Write the number or numbers.

I need more help with:

_____

_____